# Microsoft
# Purview

AI in Data Security Leveraging Microsoft Security
Copilot

Dr. Patrick Jones

OLYMPUS ACADEMY
PRESS

# TABLE OF CONTENTS

# WHY AI IS THE FUTURE OF CYBERSECURITY

Cybersecurity is in a constant state of evolution. The methods that once provided adequate protection—firewalls, antivirus software, and manual threat monitoring—are no longer enough to defend against the complexity and scale of modern cyber threats. Hackers are using automation, AI-driven attacks, and advanced social engineering tactics to bypass traditional security measures, making cyber threats more sophisticated, faster, and harder to detect than ever before.

At the same time, organizations face growing challenges in protecting their data, detecting insider threats, and ensuring compliance with evolving regulations. Security teams are drowning in alerts, struggling to differentiate between false positives and legitimate threats, and often find themselves reacting too late to prevent damage.

This is where Artificial Intelligence (AI) is changing the game. AI and machine learning are redefining how organizations detect, prevent, and respond to cyber threats, providing the speed, intelligence, and automation needed to stay ahead of attackers.

Cyber threats are no longer limited to individual hackers deploying viruses. Today's threats include:

- State-sponsored cyberattacks that use AI to automate and enhance attack capabilities.

- AI-driven phishing campaigns that mimic human interactions to deceive employees.

- Insider threats, where employees—whether accidentally or maliciously—leak sensitive data.

- Zero-day exploits, where attackers take advantage of security vulnerabilities before patches are available.

The sheer volume and complexity of cyberattacks have grown beyond human capacity to monitor and respond effectively. Organizations are flooded with security alerts every day, making it impossible for security teams to analyze and act on every incident manually.

To combat this, cybersecurity needs automation, intelligent threat detection, and real-time analysis—capabilities that AI can provide.

AI is revolutionizing cybersecurity by enhancing traditional security measures with advanced automation and intelligence. Instead of reacting to known threats, AI-driven security systems proactively detect and predict cyber risks before they escalate.

Some of AI's key roles in cybersecurity include:

- Threat detection and response – AI can scan vast amounts of data in real-time to identify patterns, anomalies, and emerging threats that humans might miss.

- Automated incident response – AI can prioritize security alerts, recommend response actions, and execute security measures faster than manual processes.

- Behavioral analytics – Machine learning enables AI to analyze user behavior, detecting unusual patterns that indicate insider threats or account takeovers.

- Security automation – AI reduces the workload on security teams by automating tasks like log analysis, compliance reporting, and policy enforcement.

AI not only makes security teams more efficient but also makes organizations more resilient against ever-evolving cyber threats.

Microsoft Security Copilot is the next step in AI-driven cybersecurity, combining the power of large-scale threat intelligence, machine learning, and automated security operations to help organizations:

- Detect threats in real-time before they cause damage.
- Automate security investigations to speed up response times.
- Provide AI-driven recommendations for risk mitigation.
- Analyze compliance gaps and enforce data protection policies across Microsoft 365 and cloud environments.

Built on Microsoft Defender, Sentinel, and Purview, Security Copilot provides centralized AI-powered security capabilities that enhance threat visibility, streamline response processes, and improve an organization's overall security posture.

With Security Copilot, organizations can move beyond reactive security measures and adopt an intelligent, proactive defense strategy.

This book is designed for:

- Security professionals who want to learn how AI can enhance their security strategy.
- IT administrators looking to automate security workflows and reduce the burden of manual monitoring.
- Compliance officers who need to ensure data security aligns with industry regulations.
- Business leaders and decision-makers interested in AI-driven security investments.

Throughout this book, we will cover:

- How Microsoft Security Copilot enhances threat detection, risk management, and compliance.
- Practical steps to integrate AI-driven security tools into your organization.
- Real-world use cases and scenarios demonstrating AI-powered cybersecurity in action.
- How to train and adapt AI security tools to fit your organization's needs.

Each chapter will provide step-by-step guidance, best practices, and insights into how AI is transforming cybersecurity.

Alex has been a security analyst for years, working in a mid-sized organization that relies on traditional cybersecurity tools like firewalls, SIEM systems, and manual log analysis. He's experienced firsthand the struggle of keeping up with thousands of daily security alerts, where distinguishing between false positives and real threats is a constant challenge.

His company has suffered multiple phishing attempts, insider security breaches, and compliance risks, forcing the security team into a reactive, firefighting mode rather than a proactive security stance.

When Alex's company decides to implement Microsoft Security Copilot, he's both excited and skeptical. Can AI really help automate security operations, detect threats faster, and improve compliance enforcement?

As he begins exploring Security Copilot's capabilities, Alex will learn how AI-driven security tools can transform an organization's security strategy—from real-time threat detection to automated incident response and adaptive risk management.

Throughout this book, we'll follow Alex's journey as he:

- Deploys Microsoft Security Copilot for the first time and configures it for his organization.

- Uses AI-driven insights to investigate security incidents faster.

- Implements automation for incident response and risk mitigation.

- Learns to balance AI-driven security with human expertise to build a strong cybersecurity defense.

By the end of the book, Alex—and you—will have a clear understanding of how AI can strengthen data security, automate threat response, and future-proof an organization's cybersecurity strategy.

AI-powered security is not just the future—it's the present. Organizations that embrace AI-driven security tools like Microsoft Security Copilot will have a competitive edge in protecting their data, detecting threats faster, and reducing security risks.

As cyber threats continue to evolve, AI will play an increasingly vital role in security operations, allowing businesses to move from reactive defenses to intelligent, proactive protection.

In the next chapter, we'll take a deep dive into Microsoft Security Copilot—what it is, how it works, and why it's changing the game for cybersecurity professionals around the world.

# CHAPTER 1: UNDERSTANDING MICROSOFT SECURITY COPILOT – THE AI-POWERED SECURITY ASSISTANT

Cybersecurity is a race against time. Every day, organizations face an overwhelming number of security threats, from phishing scams to sophisticated ransomware attacks. Security teams struggle to keep up, drowning in thousands of alerts, manually investigating potential threats, and trying to determine which incidents demand immediate action. Traditional security tools, while effective to a degree, rely on predefined rules and signatures, making them inadequate against modern, adaptive cyber threats.

This is where Microsoft Security Copilot enters the picture. As an AI-powered security assistant, it offers a new approach—one that goes beyond manual security analysis and reactive defenses. By harnessing AI-driven intelligence, Security Copilot analyzes security data in real time, detects anomalies, prioritizes high-risk threats, and automates response actions. Instead of spending hours combing through logs and trying to make sense of security alerts, security analysts can simply ask Security Copilot questions in natural language and receive clear, actionable insights instantly.

Security Copilot isn't just another security tool—it's a fundamental shift in how organizations approach cybersecurity. Built on Microsoft's extensive threat intelligence network, it integrates with Microsoft Defender, Sentinel, and Purview to provide a comprehensive security solution. It doesn't just detect threats; it learns from them, evolving alongside cybercriminal tactics to provide proactive security measures rather than reactive fixes.

For years, security teams have relied on manual investigations, static security rules, and threat signatures to detect and respond to cyber incidents. This approach works well for known threats, but as cybercriminals continue to evolve, traditional security methods often fall short. Threat actors now use automation, AI-generated phishing emails, and zero-day exploits that bypass signature-based defenses. Security teams are left trying to defend against attacks that are faster and more adaptive than their detection methods.

Security Copilot changes this by taking an AI-first approach to security operations. Instead of waiting for a predefined threat signature to match an attack, Security Copilot analyzes behavior patterns, detects anomalies, and correlates data across multiple sources to identify suspicious activity. This allows it to catch threats that traditional tools would miss, such as insider attacks, credential-based breaches, and fileless malware. It also reduces false positives by filtering out low-risk events and focusing only on critical threats, helping security teams allocate their time and resources more effectively.

Perhaps the most significant advantage of Security Copilot is its ability to automate incident response. When a security threat is detected, it doesn't just send an alert—it provides recommendations and, in some cases, takes automated action to contain the threat. This means that instead of manually triaging an incident, security analysts can rely on AI to streamline investigations, summarize security incidents, and execute response actions at machine speed.

Security Copilot brings a range of capabilities that transform how organizations approach cybersecurity. One of its primary strengths is AI-driven threat intelligence, which enables real-time analysis of vast amounts of security data. Microsoft processes trillions of security signals every day, and Security Copilot taps into this intelligence to detect emerging threats, understand attack trends, and recommend proactive security measures.

Incident investigation and response are also significantly improved with Security Copilot. Rather than having security teams manually comb through logs, it can generate attack timelines, summarize security incidents, and suggest appropriate actions to mitigate threats. For example, if an unusual login attempt is detected, Security Copilot can analyze the user's behavior history, flag the attempt as a possible credential compromise, and recommend enforcing multi-factor authentication or blocking access.

Another game-changing feature is its ability to assess risk levels in real time. Not all security threats are created equal, and Security Copilot helps security teams prioritize the most critical incidents. By providing AI-driven risk scoring and automated response recommendations, it reduces alert fatigue and allows analysts to focus on the most pressing security concerns.

Perhaps most importantly, Security Copilot seamlessly integrates with Microsoft's broader security ecosystem. It works alongside Microsoft Defender for endpoint and cloud security, Microsoft Sentinel for SIEM and SOAR capabilities, and Microsoft Purview for compliance and data protection. This ensures that security incidents are not just detected in isolation but are correlated across multiple security platforms, providing a holistic view of an organization's security posture.

Many security teams today are overwhelmed by the sheer volume of security alerts they receive. Without AI-driven filtering, most organizations waste valuable time chasing down false positives or low-priority issues, leaving them unable to respond quickly to actual security threats. Security Copilot helps by analyzing alerts in real time, identifying which incidents require immediate attention, and providing security teams with the information they need to act decisively.

Slow incident response is another significant challenge in cybersecurity. Traditional investigations can take hours—or even days—before security teams determine the scope of an attack and implement a response. Security Copilot accelerates this process by automatically generating incident summaries, tracking how threats entered a system, and recommending steps to contain and remediate the threat. This reduces response times dramatically, preventing minor security incidents from escalating into major breaches.

Advanced cyber threats, such as zero-day exploits and insider threats, also pose a significant challenge for traditional security tools. Unlike malware with a known signature, these attacks often go unnoticed until it's too late. Security Copilot's behavioral analytics capabilities allow it to detect these threats based on deviations from normal user activity, helping security teams take proactive measures to mitigate risks before they escalate.

Finally, there is the growing cybersecurity skills gap. Many organizations struggle to find skilled security professionals, leaving security teams understaffed and overworked. Security Copilot functions as an AI-powered assistant, guiding analysts through security investigations and providing step-by-step recommendations to address threats. By augmenting security teams with AI-driven insights, organizations can close the skills gap and enhance their overall security capabilities.

### Alex's Journey: Exploring Security Copilot's Capabilities for the First Time

Alex had been working in cybersecurity for years, and while he had seen many security tools come and go, he was skeptical about AI-driven security. His company had recently experienced a surge in security incidents, ranging from phishing attempts to suspicious login activity, and his team was struggling to keep up. They were receiving hundreds of security alerts each day, but distinguishing between real threats and false alarms had become a daunting task.

When his company decided to implement Microsoft Security Copilot, Alex wasn't sure what to expect. On his first day using the platform, he logged into the dashboard and typed a simple query: *"What security incidents require immediate attention?"*

Within seconds, Security Copilot generated a concise report highlighting the highest-priority threats. One incident stood out—a user had attempted to access sensitive company files from an unfamiliar location outside the country. The system provided a full attack timeline, linking data from Microsoft Defender and Sentinel to show how the login attempt correlated with other suspicious activities. Security Copilot even suggested the best course of action: blocking the account and enforcing multi-factor authentication.

What normally would have taken Alex's team hours to investigate was now resolved in minutes. For the first time, he saw how AI could dramatically improve security operations—not by replacing human analysts, but by enhancing their ability to respond quickly and effectively to real threats.

As Alex continued exploring Security Copilot's capabilities, he realized this wasn't just another security tool. It was an assistant that helped his team stay ahead of threats, automate tedious tasks, and focus on the most critical security risks. The days of being overwhelmed by endless alerts were over. Now, security decisions were smarter, faster, and more efficient.

Microsoft Security Copilot represents a shift in how organizations handle cybersecurity. By leveraging AI-driven security intelligence, it enhances threat detection, automates incident response, and provides real-time insights that empower security teams to make faster, smarter decisions.

In the next chapter, we'll explore how organizations can deploy Microsoft Security Copilot, configure its settings, and integrate it with their existing security infrastructure to maximize its effectiveness.

# CHAPTER 2: SETTING UP MICROSOFT SECURITY COPILOT FOR YOUR ORGANIZATION

Deploying Microsoft Security Copilot is more than just flipping a switch—it requires careful planning, proper licensing, and integration with existing security tools to ensure it works effectively within an organization's security infrastructure. While Security Copilot's AI-driven intelligence can dramatically improve security operations, its effectiveness depends on how well it's configured, who has access, and how it aligns with an organization's security policies.

In this chapter, we'll walk through the essential steps to set up Microsoft Security Copilot, from licensing and role-based access control to integrating it with Microsoft Defender, Sentinel, and Purview. By the end, you'll have a clear understanding of how to align AI-driven security insights with your organization's existing security strategy to maximize protection against cyber threats.

Before enabling Microsoft Security Copilot, it's essential to ensure that the organization has the right licenses and permissions. Like most enterprise security solutions from Microsoft, Security Copilot is available through specific security-focused licensing models, typically as part of Microsoft 365 E5, Microsoft Defender for Endpoint P2, or Azure-based security subscriptions.

Organizations need to verify that they have:

- A Security Copilot license assigned to the appropriate users—this is usually limited to security analysts, incident responders, and IT administrators.

- Role-based access control (RBAC) configurations to ensure only authorized personnel can view AI-generated security insights.

- Integration permissions with Microsoft Defender, Sentinel, and Purview to allow Security Copilot to pull security signals from multiple sources.

Since Security Copilot relies on analyzing data from Microsoft's security ecosystem, it works best when it has full visibility into the organization's endpoint security, cloud security, and compliance policies. Proper role-based access ensures that sensitive security insights are only available to those who need them, preventing unauthorized users from accessing or modifying security settings.

Once Security Copilot is enabled, the next step is familiarizing yourself with its dashboard and core features. Unlike traditional security interfaces that bombard analysts with logs and alerts, Security Copilot is designed to simplify security operations with AI-generated insights.

Upon logging in, security professionals will find:

- A threat intelligence feed, which provides a real-time overview of global cyber threats, security incidents, and AI-driven recommendations.

- An AI-powered query interface, where analysts can ask natural language questions like *"What are today's top security threats?"* or *"Summarize recent phishing attempts in my organization."*

- Incident summaries and automated threat reports, which allow security teams to quickly understand, prioritize, and respond to active threats without manually sifting through logs.

The AI-driven insights provided by Security Copilot are designed to reduce security investigation times, offering immediate answers, threat correlations, and response recommendations that security teams can act on right away.

Security Copilot is most effective when it pulls data from multiple security tools to provide a unified, AI-enhanced security strategy. To maximize its capabilities, organizations should integrate it with Microsoft's core security solutions:

1. Microsoft Defender – Security Copilot leverages Defender for Endpoint, Defender for Office 365, and Defender for Identity to analyze endpoint security signals, detect malware, and monitor suspicious login activity.

2. Microsoft Sentinel – Integrating with Sentinel allows Security Copilot to correlate security logs, detect anomalies, and automate security workflows for improved incident response.

3. Microsoft Purview – As organizations deal with compliance regulations like GDPR, HIPAA, and NIST, Security Copilot can pull insights from Purview's compliance monitoring tools to detect policy violations and prevent data leaks.

Integrating these tools creates a 360-degree view of an organization's security environment, enabling Security Copilot to provide context-aware threat analysis and adaptive security recommendations based on real-time activity.

While Security Copilot provides out-of-the-box AI-driven security insights, organizations must customize its configurations to align with their specific security needs and policies. Some key settings to focus on include:

- Defining AI-generated security recommendations – Organizations can fine-tune Copilot's AI models to prioritize security alerts based on their industry, compliance regulations, or specific risk factors.

- Setting automated response actions – Security teams can configure automated threat response workflows, allowing Security Copilot to block malicious activity, isolate compromised devices, or trigger security alerts without human intervention.

- Enabling compliance-based security policies – Organizations dealing with sensitive data can configure Security Copilot to detect and prevent unauthorized data transfers by enforcing data classification, encryption, and access controls.

- Establishing security reporting and auditing policies – Security Copilot can generate audit logs and compliance reports that align with organizational policies, ensuring that all security decisions are properly documented and meet industry standards.

By customizing these configurations, organizations can ensure that Security Copilot not only provides AI-driven insights but also enforces security policies in a way that aligns with business objectives and regulatory requirements.

**Alex's Journey: Configuring Security Copilot to Integrate with His Company's Security Stack**

When Alex's company decided to implement Microsoft Security Copilot, he was tasked with setting it up and ensuring it integrated smoothly with their existing security tools. As a security analyst, he had spent countless hours manually reviewing security alerts, investigating threats, and writing incident reports. The idea of using AI to automate some of these processes intrigued him—but he knew that proper setup was critical to making it work effectively.

His first step was verifying licensing and access control. He worked with his IT team to ensure that the appropriate users—himself, the security team, and IT administrators—had the necessary licenses and role-based access permissions. The last thing he wanted was for unauthorized users to access security insights that could be exploited.

Next, he logged into the Security Copilot dashboard for the first time. Unlike the overwhelming security interfaces he was used to, the AI-driven dashboard was surprisingly intuitive. Instead of being bombarded with alerts, he saw a clear summary of active threats, AI-generated insights, and a search bar where he could ask questions in plain English. Curious to test its capabilities, he typed:

*"Show me all high-priority security threats from the past 24 hours."*

Within seconds, Security Copilot provided a list of incidents, each with a risk score, AI-generated summary, and suggested next steps. One particular threat caught Alex's attention—an unauthorized login attempt from an employee's account in another country. The AI suggested enabling multi-factor authentication (MFA) for the user and reviewing their access logs to see if any sensitive data had been compromised.

Realizing the potential of Security Copilot, Alex moved on to integrating it with Microsoft Defender and Sentinel. Once connected, the AI could correlate security alerts across endpoints, cloud services, and email traffic, providing a much clearer picture of potential threats. The next time his team received a phishing alert, Security Copilot automatically generated an attack timeline, showing how the email had been sent, which users interacted with it, and whether any malicious payloads had been executed.

By the end of the day, Alex was convinced—Security Copilot was going to revolutionize how his team handled security investigations. Instead of sifting through logs and manually investigating threats, they could ask the AI questions, get instant insights, and focus on acting rather than analyzing.

Setting up Microsoft Security Copilot is a crucial first step in leveraging AI to enhance cybersecurity operations. Ensuring proper licensing, integrating security tools, and customizing configurations allows organizations to maximize the AI's ability to detect, analyze, and respond to threats efficiently.

In the next chapter, we'll explore how AI-driven threat detection works in Security Copilot, how it identifies suspicious behavior, and how it helps security teams stay ahead of cyber threats before they escalate.

# CHAPTER 3: AI-POWERED THREAT DETECTION AND RISK INTELLIGENCE

Modern cyber threats are evolving at an unprecedented pace, outpacing traditional security methods and leaving organizations vulnerable to advanced attacks, insider threats, and data breaches. Conventional security tools rely heavily on signature-based detection, which means they can only identify known threats. This approach, while effective against common malware and phishing attempts, fails when attackers use new techniques, zero-day exploits, or adaptive attack strategies.

Artificial intelligence (AI) is transforming cybersecurity by enabling real-time threat detection, predictive risk analysis, and automated response strategies. With AI-driven security tools, organizations can proactively identify and mitigate threats before they escalate, rather than reacting after the damage is done.

Microsoft Security Copilot brings these capabilities to life by analyzing vast amounts of security data, correlating information across multiple sources, and identifying patterns that indicate malicious activity. In this chapter, we'll explore how AI-powered threat detection works, how Security Copilot improves risk intelligence, and how it helps security teams stay ahead of cybercriminals.

Traditional security tools operate based on predefined rules and known threat signatures, which means they can only detect attacks that match previously identified patterns. This reactive approach leaves organizations vulnerable to:

- Zero-day exploits, where attackers take advantage of newly discovered vulnerabilities before they are patched.
- Fileless malware, which executes in memory rather than being installed as a traditional executable file, making it harder to detect.

- Insider threats, where employees or contractors misuse their access to steal, leak, or manipulate sensitive data.

AI-driven security tools take a different approach, using behavioral analysis and anomaly detection to identify threats before they escalate. By analyzing normal user behavior and system activity, AI can detect deviations that might indicate a security threat, even if the specific attack method has never been seen before.

For example, Security Copilot can identify when a user suddenly begins accessing sensitive files at unusual hours, logging in from an unfamiliar location, or transferring large amounts of data outside the organization. These patterns might not match a known attack, but the AI recognizes them as suspicious and automatically flags them for further investigation.

Machine learning plays a crucial role in identifying patterns of malicious behavior that traditional security methods might overlook. Unlike rule-based detection, which operates on static if-then conditions, machine learning continuously adapts and learns from new data to improve its accuracy over time.

Security Copilot leverages machine learning to:

- Monitor user behavior across Microsoft 365 applications and flag anomalies such as unauthorized data access or privilege escalation.

- Analyze endpoint activity in Microsoft Defender to detect when devices exhibit malware-like behavior without relying on traditional virus signatures.

- Correlate authentication patterns in Microsoft Entra ID (formerly Azure AD) to detect potential compromised accounts based on login anomalies.

For example, an employee suddenly downloading thousands of confidential files before resigning might not trigger an alert in traditional security tools. But Security Copilot, recognizing the deviation from normal behavior, detects this as a possible insider threat and automatically raises a security alert.

Machine learning also helps reduce false positives by distinguishing between benign anomalies and real threats. This allows security teams to focus on high-priority incidents rather than wasting time investigating routine deviations.

One of the most significant advantages of Security Copilot is its ability to correlate security data from multiple sources to detect threats that might otherwise go unnoticed. Cyberattacks rarely occur in isolation; they often involve multiple attack vectors, such as phishing emails, compromised endpoints, and unauthorized cloud access.

Security Copilot aggregates and analyzes data from:

- Microsoft Defender for Endpoint, which monitors device activity and detects malware, ransomware, and suspicious processes.

- Microsoft Defender for Office 365, which scans incoming emails for phishing attempts, malicious attachments, and impersonation attacks.

- Microsoft Sentinel, which collects security logs from across the organization to provide a centralized threat detection system.

By cross-referencing events from these different security tools, Security Copilot can identify connections that humans might miss.

For example, suppose an attacker sends a phishing email to an employee, who then clicks on a malicious link and unknowingly downloads malware. Traditional security tools might detect this as an isolated incident. However, Security Copilot can correlate the email event with endpoint activity and network traffic to:

1. Identify that the employee clicked on a malicious link from an external sender.

2. Detect that their device then began communicating with an unusual external IP address.

3. Flag that the same compromised device attempted to access sensitive company data shortly afterward.

Instead of treating each event separately, Security Copilot links them together, providing security teams with a complete picture of the attack and recommending response actions to contain it.

Security Copilot doesn't just analyze past incidents—it also helps organizations anticipate and prevent future attacks using threat intelligence. Microsoft continuously collects trillions of security signals from across the globe, feeding this data into Security Copilot's AI models to help organizations understand:

- Which attack techniques are trending and how cybercriminals are evolving their tactics.

- Which vulnerabilities are being actively exploited, allowing organizations to prioritize patching efforts.

- Which industries and geographies are being targeted, helping businesses assess their risk exposure.

By using AI-driven threat intelligence, Security Copilot can alert security teams to potential risks before they impact the organization. For instance, if Security Copilot detects that a new form of ransomware is spreading globally, it can:

- Assess whether the organization is vulnerable to the exploit based on its security configuration.

- Automatically recommend security patches and endpoint protection settings to mitigate the risk.

- Implement proactive security measures, such as blocking suspicious domains associated with the attack.

This predictive approach shifts security from reactive to proactive, allowing organizations to stay ahead of cyber threats rather than merely responding to them.

**Alex's Journey: Investigating a Suspicious Activity Alert with AI-Powered Insights**

Alex had seen his fair share of security alerts, but most of them required hours of investigation before he could determine if they were genuine threats. His team often found themselves stuck in a cycle of chasing false positives while missing actual security incidents.

One morning, he logged into Microsoft Security Copilot and immediately saw an AI-generated alert for unusual login activity. The alert summary indicated that a user had accessed company data from an unusual location in another country, despite no record of previous travel from that employee. Normally, Alex would have needed to dig through multiple security logs to piece together the full story, but Security Copilot had already correlated data from Microsoft Defender, Sentinel, and Entra ID to build a complete attack timeline.

The AI-generated report revealed:

- The login attempt originated from an IP address associated with a known botnet.

- The attacker had used a valid set of employee credentials, suggesting a potential account compromise.

- The same credentials had been used to attempt a high-volume data transfer shortly after login.

Instead of spending hours manually reviewing logs, Alex now had everything he needed in seconds. Security Copilot recommended an immediate response: blocking the login, resetting the user's password, and enforcing multi-factor authentication to prevent further unauthorized access.

For the first time, Alex felt like he had a security assistant that worked alongside him rather than just another tool generating alerts. The AI had done the investigative legwork, allowing him to act quickly to prevent a potential data breach.

AI-powered threat detection is revolutionizing cybersecurity, allowing organizations to identify and respond to threats faster and more effectively than ever before. Security Copilot brings together machine learning, behavioral analytics, and real-time threat intelligence to help security teams stay ahead of cybercriminals.

In the next chapter, we'll explore how AI-driven automation streamlines incident response, reduces investigation time, and enables security teams to act on threats with unprecedented speed and efficiency.

# CHAPTER 4: AUTOMATING INCIDENT RESPONSE WITH MICROSOFT SECURITY COPILOT

Cybersecurity incidents are often a race against time. The longer a threat remains undetected or unaddressed, the greater the potential damage. Whether it's a phishing attack, a ransomware infection, or an insider threat, security teams must act quickly to contain the incident, prevent data loss, and protect critical systems. However, traditional incident response methods often rely on manual processes, leading to delays that attackers can exploit.

This is where AI-driven automation is transforming security operations. Microsoft Security Copilot enhances incident response by automating threat detection, investigation, and containment, significantly reducing the time it takes for security teams to react to threats. Instead of waiting for analysts to manually correlate logs, investigate alerts, and determine the next steps, Security Copilot provides real-time remediation recommendations and automated response workflows, ensuring threats are addressed as soon as they emerge.

In this chapter, we'll explore how Security Copilot streamlines incident response, reduces human effort, and improves organizational security posture through AI-driven automation.

Security operations teams (SecOps) are under constant pressure to keep up with an overwhelming volume of alerts. The traditional approach to incident response involves several time-consuming steps:

1. Detecting a security event – Security tools generate alerts based on suspicious activity.

2. Investigating the incident – Security analysts review logs, correlate data, and determine if an actual threat is present.

25

3. Containing the threat – Once confirmed, actions such as isolating affected endpoints, revoking compromised credentials, or blocking malicious IPs must be taken.

4. Remediating the issue – Patching vulnerabilities, restoring lost data, or implementing long-term security measures to prevent recurrence.

Each of these steps traditionally requires human intervention, slowing down response times and increasing the risk of a successful attack. AI-driven automation removes bottlenecks, allowing security teams to act faster and more efficiently.

Security Copilot plays a critical role in automating these security operations by:

- Detecting and prioritizing security incidents automatically.

- Generating detailed attack timelines to aid investigation.

- Recommending and executing response actions in real time.

Instead of waiting for a security analyst to manually investigate, AI-driven security tools can contain threats automatically, ensuring organizations don't waste valuable time.

One of the most powerful features of Security Copilot is its ability to automate security workflows, allowing organizations to define pre-configured response actions for different types of incidents. These workflows help teams contain threats before they escalate, reducing the need for constant human oversight.

For example, security teams can configure workflows to:

- Automatically block user accounts if suspicious login activity is detected from an unusual location.

- Isolate infected endpoints if ransomware or malware is detected.

- Quarantine phishing emails if flagged as high risk by Security Copilot.

These automated workflows streamline security response, ensuring that high-priority threats are addressed instantly while freeing up security teams to focus on more complex investigations.

Security Copilot enhances incident response by providing:

1. Instant Threat Summaries – Instead of manually reviewing security alerts, analysts can ask Security Copilot questions like:

    o *"Summarize the last five security incidents."*

    o *"What actions have been taken to contain a detected threat?"*

    o *"Show me the attack timeline for a recent phishing attempt."*

Within seconds, Security Copilot analyzes logs, correlates security signals, and presents a clear summary of the threat.

2. Automated Attack Timelines – Security Copilot visualizes the sequence of events in a security incident, helping analysts understand how an attack unfolded and what actions need to be taken next.

3. Real-Time Remediation Actions – Instead of waiting for human intervention, Security Copilot can be configured to execute response actions automatically, such as:

    o Blocking a compromised user account.

    o Isolating a device that shows signs of malware infection.

    o Alerting security teams to initiate additional investigations.

By removing manual steps from the process, Security Copilot enables security teams to respond to threats in real time rather than after the damage has already occurred.

For years, security teams have been burdened by alert fatigue, spending hours investigating low-priority threats while struggling to keep up with high-risk incidents. AI-driven automation removes this workload, allowing security teams to:

- Focus on critical security risks rather than getting overwhelmed by unnecessary alerts.

- Reduce false positives by letting AI prioritize real threats over non-urgent issues.

- Eliminate repetitive tasks like reviewing log files or manually blocking suspicious IPs.

Security Copilot ensures that security teams spend their time where it matters most—on strategy, threat hunting, and improving security posture—rather than drowning in alerts and manual processes.


**Alex's Journey: Using Security Copilot to Respond to a Phishing Attack in Minutes**

Alex had handled dozens of phishing incidents over the years, but each one followed a frustratingly slow process. The team would receive a report about a suspicious email, manually review email logs, determine who had interacted with the message, and then check whether any credentials had been compromised. By the time they acted, the attacker had often already gained access.

One morning, Alex logged into Security Copilot and saw an AI-generated alert for a high-risk phishing attempt. The AI had already analyzed email metadata, user activity, and security logs to determine that multiple employees had received and clicked on a phishing email disguised as an internal IT message.

Before Alex even had a chance to start his usual investigation, Security Copilot had already correlated the attack timeline and provided recommended response actions:

1. Quarantine the email across all inboxes.

2. Revoke session tokens for affected users to prevent further account access.

3. Enforce multi-factor authentication (MFA) for the compromised accounts.

4. Block the sender's domain across Microsoft Defender for Office 365.

Alex didn't have to spend hours piecing the information together— Security Copilot had done the investigative work for him. With a few clicks, he confirmed the recommended actions, and within minutes, the phishing threat was neutralized.

Feeling a mix of relief and amazement, Alex realized that this was what cybersecurity should feel like—not chasing alerts, not struggling to investigate every suspicious email manually, but having an AI-powered assistant that worked alongside his team to take action quickly and efficiently.

With Security Copilot handling low-level security investigations and automating response workflows, Alex's team had more time to focus on proactive security measures, like employee training and advanced threat hunting. For the first time in his career, incident response didn't feel like firefighting—it felt like being ahead of the game.

Automating incident response is one of the biggest advantages of AI-driven security. Security Copilot removes delays, streamlines security workflows, and ensures that threats are neutralized in real time. Instead of waiting for analysts to investigate every alert manually, AI-powered automation executes rapid containment actions, keeping organizations protected even when security teams are stretched thin.

In the next chapter, we'll explore how AI enhances insider risk detection, identifies behavioral anomalies, and prevents data exfiltration before it happens.

# CHAPTER 5: ENHANCING INSIDER RISK DETECTION WITH AI

Insider threats pose one of the most significant security risks to organizations. Unlike external attacks, which often rely on breaking through firewalls and security measures, insider threats come from trusted individuals who already have access to sensitive systems and data. Whether an employee is intentionally stealing company information, accidentally exposing confidential data, or being manipulated by external attackers, the results can be devastating.

Traditional security tools struggle to detect insider threats because they focus on external threats and perimeter defenses. However, AI-driven security solutions like Microsoft Security Copilot offer a more effective approach. By analyzing user behavior, identifying anomalies, and detecting data movement patterns, AI can flag suspicious activity before it turns into a full-blown security incident.

In this chapter, we'll explore how AI enhances insider risk detection, how Security Copilot uses behavioral analytics to identify potential threats, and how automated risk detection prevents unauthorized data exfiltration before it happens.

Not all insider threats are malicious—in fact, many security incidents stem from careless mistakes or poor security awareness. Understanding the different types of insider threats is crucial for applying the right security controls.

1. Malicious Insiders – These are employees, contractors, or business partners who intentionally steal data, sabotage systems, or misuse their access for personal or financial gain. This can include selling intellectual property, leaking confidential customer data, or planting backdoors for later exploitation.

2. Negligent Insiders – Employees who accidentally expose sensitive information through poor security practices, weak passwords, or careless data sharing. Examples include sending confidential documents to the wrong recipient, failing to encrypt files, or using personal email accounts for work-related tasks.

3. Compromised Insiders – Even well-intentioned employees can become security risks if their credentials are stolen or their accounts are hijacked by cybercriminals. In many cases, attackers use phishing, credential stuffing, or malware to gain access to an insider's account and impersonate them.

Traditional security tools often fail to differentiate between normal and suspicious behavior, making it difficult to detect insider risks. AI changes the game by analyzing user behavior, identifying high-risk actions, and applying automated security controls to prevent data leaks.

One of the most powerful aspects of AI in security is its ability to learn normal behavior and identify deviations. Security Copilot continuously monitors user activity across Microsoft 365 apps, endpoints, and cloud services, looking for signs that an employee may be acting suspiciously.

For example, AI can detect when:

- An employee who never downloads large files suddenly exports gigabytes of data from a SharePoint site.

- A user accesses confidential documents outside of their normal work hours or from an unfamiliar location.

- An account that typically logs in from a single office location suddenly starts accessing resources from multiple geographic regions within hours.

By using machine learning models, Security Copilot doesn't just rely on predefined rules—it continuously adapts to new behavioral trends, improving its ability to detect real insider risks while minimizing false positives.

When unusual data access patterns are detected, Security Copilot can:

- Flag the activity for review by security teams.

- Trigger additional authentication requirements, such as multi-factor authentication (MFA).

- Automatically restrict access to sensitive files or applications until further verification is completed.

This proactive approach to insider risk detection allows security teams to respond before serious damage occurs.

Not all security threats require immediate account lockdowns or drastic actions. Many insider risk scenarios involve gray areas—for instance, an employee might be accessing an unusually large amount of data but has a legitimate business reason for doing so.

AI-powered adaptive security controls allow Security Copilot to apply risk-based security measures based on the severity of a user's behavior. These controls can:

- Apply stricter security policies dynamically when a user exhibits risky behavior.

- Restrict high-risk file transfers, such as downloading financial records to personal devices.

- Alert managers or security personnel when an employee attempts to access sensitive data outside of their normal scope.

For example, if an employee who usually works in the marketing department suddenly tries to access HR salary reports, Security Copilot doesn't automatically block the request—instead, it may:

- Require additional authentication before allowing access.

- Send an alert to HR or IT security to review the request.

- Temporarily restrict document downloads until further verification is completed.

This context-aware approach ensures that genuine security threats are stopped, while legitimate business activities are not disrupted.

One of the biggest security risks that organizations face is data exfiltration, where employees intentionally or unintentionally transfer confidential data to external locations. Security Copilot's automated risk detection system helps prevent data leaks by:

- Monitoring file transfers to external email addresses, USB drives, or cloud storage providers like Google Drive and Dropbox.

- Blocking unauthorized data transfers in real-time and alerting security teams.

- Detecting patterns of excessive data movement, such as an employee emailing dozens of confidential files within a short period.

If Security Copilot detects a high-risk data transfer, it can automatically revoke access to the affected files, quarantine the employee's session, and prevent further unauthorized downloads until the security team completes an investigation.

By applying real-time protections, Security Copilot ensures that sensitive data stays within the organization and is not exposed to unauthorized individuals.


**Alex's Journey: Discovering an Unauthorized Data Transfer Before It Became a Security Incident**

Alex had seen his fair share of insider threats—both intentional and accidental. But detecting them in time had always been a challenge. Many times, by the time his security team realized a data breach had occurred, the damage was already done.

One afternoon, Alex was reviewing his Security Copilot dashboard when an AI-generated alert caught his attention. The alert indicated that an employee had attempted to email a confidential financial report to a personal email address—an unusual activity for someone in their role.

Rather than having to manually investigate multiple security logs, Security Copilot had already compiled a complete summary of the incident:

- The employee had accessed multiple financial reports outside of normal business hours.

- They had attempted to download large amounts of data before sending an email to their personal Gmail account.

- This behavior deviated significantly from the employee's typical work patterns, marking it as high-risk.

Before Alex even needed to take action, Security Copilot had already blocked the email from being sent and restricted the employee's access to further downloads. The system automatically flagged the incident for further review, ensuring that Alex's team could investigate before data was lost.

Following up on the case, Alex met with HR and the employee's manager to determine if the data transfer had been an accident or a deliberate attempt at data theft. The employee, as it turned out, had recently accepted a job offer at another company and was attempting to take confidential reports before leaving.

Thanks to Security Copilot, the data was never compromised, and Alex's team was able to prevent a serious security breach before it happened.

As Alex reflected on the incident, he realized just how much Security Copilot had transformed insider risk detection. What once required hours of investigation was now handled automatically, ensuring that insider threats were detected, investigated, and stopped in real time.

Insider threats remain one of the biggest security challenges for organizations, but AI-driven solutions like Security Copilot provide a new level of protection. By using behavioral analytics, adaptive security controls, and real-time risk detection, Security Copilot ensures that insider threats are detected early and prevented before they can cause harm.

In the next chapter, we'll explore how AI helps organizations meet compliance requirements, automate regulatory reporting, and ensure data security aligns with industry standards.

# CHAPTER 6: AI AND COMPLIANCE – ENSURING REGULATORY READINESS

Meeting compliance requirements is a constant challenge for organizations. Regulations like GDPR, HIPAA, and NIST set strict guidelines for how data should be stored, processed, and protected. However, keeping up with compliance obligations can be overwhelming, especially when security teams are already managing daily cyber threats, insider risks, and incident response efforts.

Traditionally, compliance monitoring involves lengthy manual audits, extensive documentation, and ongoing risk assessments. Security teams must ensure that policies are enforced, data protection controls are in place, and security incidents are properly reported. Failure to comply can result in severe penalties, legal consequences, and reputational damage.

This is where AI-driven compliance tools like Microsoft Security Copilot provide a game-changing advantage. By automating compliance monitoring, generating security reports, and offering AI-driven recommendations, Security Copilot helps organizations stay ahead of regulatory requirements with minimal manual effort.

In this chapter, we'll explore how AI simplifies compliance monitoring, automates security audits, strengthens risk assessments, and ensures regulatory readiness across the organization.

One of the biggest challenges in regulatory compliance is maintaining visibility into security controls and policies. Many organizations struggle with:

- Tracking which compliance frameworks they adhere to and ensuring they meet all requirements.
- Monitoring security configurations across Microsoft 365, Azure, and other cloud environments.

- Generating detailed compliance reports for auditors and regulators.

AI simplifies compliance monitoring by continuously analyzing an organization's security posture, detecting gaps in compliance, and automatically suggesting corrective actions.

Security Copilot provides real-time compliance insights, allowing security teams to:

- Identify security misconfigurations before they become compliance violations.

- Monitor compliance across multiple frameworks (GDPR, HIPAA, ISO 27001, NIST).

- Generate audit-ready compliance reports in seconds.

Instead of manually tracking compliance status across spreadsheets and reports, organizations can rely on AI-driven insights to maintain continuous compliance visibility.

Security audits are critical for ensuring that an organization remains compliant, but they are often time-consuming, resource-intensive, and prone to human error. Organizations must regularly conduct internal audits, third-party assessments, and compliance reviews to ensure they are following regulatory guidelines.

Security Copilot streamlines security audits by automating key processes, including:

- Identifying security risks that could lead to compliance violations.

- Assessing data protection policies and access controls.

- Detecting security misconfigurations that violate compliance requirements.

For example, if an organization is preparing for a GDPR audit, Security Copilot can:

- Analyze access logs to ensure that sensitive customer data is protected.
- Check encryption policies to confirm compliance with GDPR's data protection requirements.
- Generate a report detailing any areas that need remediation before the official audit.

By automating security assessments and compliance checks, AI-driven tools help organizations reduce the burden of audits while ensuring regulatory readiness.

Compliance isn't just about checking boxes—it's about ensuring that data protection policies align with real-world security threats. Security Copilot helps organizations strengthen their compliance posture by providing AI-driven recommendations tailored to their unique security risks.

For example, if an organization is struggling with data access control issues, Security Copilot might recommend:

- Enforcing role-based access policies to restrict sensitive data to authorized users only.
- Enabling multi-factor authentication (MFA) for high-risk accounts.
- Applying sensitivity labels to classify and protect confidential information.

If an organization handles healthcare data and must comply with HIPAA, Security Copilot can:

- Detect unauthorized access to patient records and alert security teams.
- Recommend stronger encryption policies to protect electronic health information.
- Automate compliance reporting to ensure all security incidents are properly documented.

By leveraging AI-driven insights, organizations can proactively address security risks and maintain a stronger, more resilient compliance posture.

Risk assessments play a crucial role in identifying vulnerabilities and ensuring that security policies are aligned with compliance standards. Many organizations struggle with:

- Manually assessing risks across multiple security systems.

- Understanding the impact of security misconfigurations on compliance.

- Prioritizing which risks to address first.

Security Copilot streamlines risk assessments by automatically identifying high-risk areas and providing prioritized recommendations. It can:

- Analyze user activity and detect compliance violations, such as unauthorized access to sensitive data.

- Identify misconfigured security settings that could lead to compliance gaps.

- Generate a risk score for each compliance-related issue, helping security teams focus on the most critical risks first.

Instead of manually reviewing security logs and policy settings, security teams can rely on AI-driven compliance insights to make faster, more informed decisions.

### Alex's Journey: Preparing His Company for an Internal Compliance Audit Using AI-Driven Tools

Alex had been through compliance audits before, and he knew how stressful they could be. The process typically involved weeks of gathering documentation, reviewing security policies, and manually checking configurations to ensure that the company met all necessary regulations.

When his company's compliance team announced an upcoming internal audit, Alex decided to use Security Copilot to streamline the process.

His first step was to ask Security Copilot for a compliance overview: *"Show me any security misconfigurations that could lead to compliance violations."*

Within seconds, the AI-generated report highlighted several issues, including:

- Inactive accounts that still had access to sensitive financial records.

- A SharePoint site containing unprotected confidential documents.

- An outdated encryption policy that did not meet the latest security standards.

Instead of manually reviewing each issue, Alex followed Security Copilot's recommendations:

- Revoked access for inactive accounts to reduce insider risk.

- Applied Sensitivity Labels to protect confidential documents in SharePoint.

- Updated the encryption settings to align with the latest compliance requirements.

Next, he used Security Copilot to generate an audit-ready compliance report that summarized:

- The company's current security posture.

- Any policy improvements that had been made.

- Recommended next steps to ensure full compliance.

When the internal auditors arrived, Alex's team was fully prepared, with all necessary security documentation and a clear risk assessment report. Instead of scrambling to gather last-minute details, they had AI-powered insights that simplified the entire process.

Reflecting on the experience, Alex realized that compliance audits didn't have to be a headache anymore. With Security Copilot's automated compliance monitoring and AI-driven recommendations, his team could stay audit-ready year-round—not just when an audit was scheduled.

Compliance management is a critical responsibility for security teams, but it doesn't have to be an overwhelming process. AI-driven tools like Security Copilot automate compliance monitoring, risk assessments, and security audits, ensuring that organizations stay ahead of regulatory requirements with minimal effort.

By leveraging real-time compliance insights and AI-driven recommendations, organizations can reduce compliance risks, streamline audit preparations, and strengthen their overall security posture.

In the next chapter, we'll explore how AI helps organizations predict and mitigate future cyber threats using proactive security intelligence and real-time threat analysis.

# CHAPTER 7: STRENGTHENING DATA LOSS PREVENTION (DLP) WITH AI

Preventing data leaks and unauthorized sharing of sensitive information is one of the most critical aspects of cybersecurity. Organizations must ensure that confidential business data, intellectual property, and regulated information are protected from both accidental exposure and intentional data theft.

Traditional Data Loss Prevention (DLP) solutions rely on predefined rules to prevent unauthorized sharing of sensitive data. However, these static rules often lead to false positives, excessive restrictions, and limited adaptability to evolving threats. This is where AI-driven DLP solutions, powered by Microsoft Security Copilot, significantly enhance an organization's ability to detect, prevent, and respond to data security risks.

By leveraging AI-powered insights, real-time monitoring, and automated policy enforcement, Security Copilot ensures that DLP policies are dynamic, adaptive, and proactive.

In this chapter, we'll explore how AI strengthens DLP policies, prevents unauthorized data transfers, and automates security enforcement to mitigate data security risks.

DLP policies are designed to protect sensitive data from being shared, downloaded, or transmitted outside of an organization's security boundaries. Traditional DLP solutions often rely on keyword-based filtering and predefined security rules, which can be inflexible and prone to misclassification.

AI-driven DLP, on the other hand, analyzes context, user behavior, and intent to determine whether a data transfer is truly a security risk. By integrating with Microsoft 365's security ecosystem, Security Copilot enhances DLP policies by:

- Using machine learning models to recognize sensitive data beyond simple keyword detection.

- Analyzing past user behavior to differentiate between normal business activities and potential data exfiltration.

- Applying real-time risk scoring to assess whether a specific data-sharing attempt is malicious, negligent, or accidental.

For example, an employee sharing a financial report with a trusted colleague is not the same as sending that report to a personal email account or uploading it to an unauthorized cloud service. AI-driven DLP policies adapt to real-world business scenarios, ensuring that legitimate workflows aren't interrupted, while security risks are immediately flagged.

One of the biggest challenges in data security is the timing of detection and enforcement. In traditional DLP solutions, violations are often identified after data has already been shared, leaving security teams scrambling to contain the damage.

With AI-enhanced DLP policies, Security Copilot can:

- Analyze data-sharing attempts in real-time and block high-risk transfers immediately.

- Detect when sensitive files are being moved to unauthorized locations (e.g., external USB drives, personal cloud storage, or email accounts).

- Apply automated security measures based on the risk level of the detected behavior.

For example, if an employee tries to upload a database of customer records to an unauthorized cloud service, Security Copilot:

- Instantly flags the transfer as high-risk.

- Blocks the upload before any data leaves the organization.

- Notifies the security team and logs the event for further investigation.

This proactive approach ensures that data breaches are prevented before they happen, rather than simply reacting after the fact.

One of the key advantages of AI-powered security solutions is their ability to identify behavioral patterns and detect anomalies. Security Copilot continuously monitors:

- Who is accessing sensitive data and how frequently.

- Where sensitive data is being shared (internally vs. externally).

- Whether an employee's data-sharing behavior has changed (e.g., downloading large amounts of data before resigning).

This behavioral analysis allows Security Copilot to detect early warning signs of a potential data breach, even when there are no clear policy violations yet.

For instance, if an employee:

- Suddenly downloads hundreds of sensitive files after receiving a job offer at a competitor, Security Copilot can flag this activity for review.

- Begins sharing confidential reports with external contacts they've never interacted with before, the system can automatically restrict further sharing until an investigation is completed.

By continuously learning from real-world user behavior, Security Copilot ensures that data security policies remain adaptive and effective.

AI-driven DLP automation reduces the burden on security teams by automatically enforcing policies, blocking unauthorized transfers, and escalating high-risk incidents.

Security Copilot automates three key areas of enforcement:

1. Blocking Unauthorized Data Transfers: If a user attempts to email confidential reports to an external recipient, Security Copilot automatically prevents the email from being sent and notifies IT security.

2. Applying Risk-Based Access Controls: If a high-risk user (such as someone flagged for insider risk) tries to copy sensitive data to a personal device, Security Copilot revokes their access immediately.

3. Escalating Critical Incidents: If multiple security violations occur within a short timeframe, Security Copilot prioritizes them for investigation, ensuring that security teams focus on the most urgent threats first.

This level of automation ensures that DLP enforcement is consistent, immediate, and scalable, allowing organizations to secure their sensitive data without slowing down productivity.

## Alex's Journey: Preventing a Major Data Leak with AI-Powered DLP Policies

Alex had spent years working in cybersecurity, and he knew how difficult it was to prevent data leaks without disrupting business operations. Employees needed to share information to do their jobs effectively, but excessive restrictions often led to frustration and workarounds—which, ironically, created even greater security risks.

One morning, Alex received an AI-generated alert from Security Copilot. A financial analyst had attempted to send a set of confidential company reports to their personal email. Normally, this kind of incident would have required manual investigation, log analysis, and hours of security review. But this time, Security Copilot had already:

- Blocked the email from being sent, preventing the data from leaving the company.

- Analyzed the employee's recent activity, revealing that they had also downloaded multiple sensitive files to a USB drive in the past 24 hours.

- Identified that the employee had recently submitted their resignation, marking them as a higher-risk individual for potential data exfiltration.

Instead of scrambling to piece together the full story, Alex had everything he needed in seconds. He immediately contacted HR and the employee's manager, who confirmed that the analyst had accepted a job at a competing firm.

With Security Copilot's AI-powered DLP policies, Alex was able to stop a potential data breach before it happened. Without this level of automation, the data could have been leaked before security teams even realized what was happening.

Reflecting on the incident, Alex realized that AI wasn't just enhancing data security—it was completely changing the game. Instead of playing defense, his security team was now proactively preventing threats, protecting data, and keeping the company secure in real time.


Data Loss Prevention is a critical component of modern cybersecurity, but traditional DLP solutions often struggle to balance security with usability. AI-driven solutions like Microsoft Security Copilot offer a smarter, more adaptive approach to data protection, ensuring that organizations can:

- Detect and block unauthorized data transfers in real time.
- Monitor risky user behaviors and prevent insider threats.
- Automate policy enforcement, reducing the workload on security teams.

By leveraging AI-powered insights and automated security controls, organizations can strengthen their data protection strategies without slowing down business operations.

In the next chapter, we'll explore how AI helps organizations predict and mitigate future cyber threats using proactive security intelligence and real-time threat analysis.

# CHAPTER 8: REDUCING SECURITY ALERT FATIGUE WITH AI-POWERED INSIGHTS

Cybersecurity teams are constantly under pressure. With the growing number of cyber threats, security analysts are drowning in alerts, many of which turn out to be false positives or low-priority incidents. Instead of focusing on actual security risks, teams often find themselves chasing alerts that don't require immediate attention while potentially missing real threats buried in the noise.

This overwhelming volume of alerts—commonly known as alert fatigue—has become one of the biggest challenges for modern security operations centers (SOCs). The problem isn't just the number of alerts; it's the lack of prioritization. Analysts have to manually sort through logs, verify incidents, and determine which threats need immediate action, creating slow response times and an increased risk of security breaches.

This is where AI-powered security solutions like Microsoft Security Copilot bring a much-needed transformation. By automating threat prioritization, reducing false positives, and summarizing incidents with AI-driven insights, Security Copilot enables security teams to focus on the threats that matter most.

In this chapter, we'll explore how AI helps reduce security alert fatigue, improves incident response efficiency, and ensures that SOCs operate at peak performance.

Security teams today receive thousands of alerts daily from various sources, including:

- Microsoft Defender for Endpoint detecting suspicious file executions.

- Microsoft Sentinel flagging unusual login attempts.

- Email security solutions identifying potential phishing attempts.

- Cloud security platforms tracking anomalous data transfers.

Many of these alerts are false positives—legitimate activities that get flagged due to overly strict security rules. Others are low-priority incidents that don't require immediate action, but still consume valuable analyst time.

This flood of alerts leads to several major problems:

- Delayed response to real security threats because teams are busy triaging minor incidents.

- Burnout among security analysts, leading to high turnover rates in SOC teams.

- Critical security incidents slipping through the cracks due to lack of prioritization.

Without a way to intelligently filter and rank security alerts, SOCs remain overloaded, reactive, and vulnerable.

Security Copilot introduces AI-driven intelligence to filter out low-risk alerts and highlight the most critical security threats. Instead of treating all alerts equally, it:

- Analyzes incident context to determine whether a threat is real or a false positive.

- Correlates multiple security signals to detect patterns that indicate a more serious attack.

- Ranks incidents by severity, ensuring that security teams focus on the highest-risk threats first.

For example, rather than simply alerting on anomalous login attempts, Security Copilot correlates multiple factors:

- Is this login attempt from a high-risk country?

- Has this user recently had their credentials exposed in a breach?

- Is there a pattern of failed login attempts before this successful one?

By considering these factors, Security Copilot can determine whether the login attempt is likely an actual attack or just a harmless travel-related login change. This reduces false positives and ensures that security teams spend their time on real threats, not routine deviations.

One of the most powerful aspects of Security Copilot is threat scoring, where AI assigns a risk level to each security incident based on real-time data analysis.

Instead of presenting analysts with an endless list of security alerts, Security Copilot:

- Ranks threats based on urgency, assigning each incident a low, medium, or high-risk score.

- Explains why an incident was flagged, offering an AI-generated summary of potential attack patterns.

- Suggests appropriate next steps, such as isolating a device, enforcing multi-factor authentication, or blocking a malicious domain.

By automating threat scoring and response recommendations, Security Copilot helps security analysts act faster and more decisively, ensuring that the most dangerous threats are contained before they escalate.

One of the biggest time-wasters in security operations is manually investigating alerts. Traditional security tools often require analysts to dig through logs, correlate events, and piece together a timeline of what happened.

Security Copilot eliminates this inefficiency by automating alert triage and generating instant incident summaries. When a security event occurs, analysts can simply ask Security Copilot:

- *"Summarize the last five high-risk security incidents."*

- *"Show me all suspicious login attempts in the past 24 hours."*

- *"Explain why this user's account is flagged as compromised."*

Within seconds, Security Copilot provides a full incident timeline, identifies root causes, and recommends remediation actions, allowing security teams to:

- Resolve security threats in minutes rather than hours.

- Reduce manual investigation workloads.

- Focus on proactive threat hunting instead of reactive triage.

By integrating automated triage with AI-generated insights, Security Copilot ensures that SOCs operate efficiently and effectively.

## Alex's Journey: Streamlining His Security Team's Workload with AI-Driven Threat Prioritization

Alex had been managing a growing security team, and one of the biggest challenges they faced was keeping up with security alerts. His team was constantly reacting, struggling to differentiate between real threats and false alarms.

On a particularly stressful day, the SOC received hundreds of alerts about suspicious login attempts across multiple user accounts. Normally, this would have taken hours of manual investigation, cross-checking logs, and verifying whether the login attempts were legitimate or actual security incidents.

But this time, Security Copilot handled it differently.

Instead of manually sorting through the alerts, Alex asked Security Copilot:

*"Prioritize the top security threats from today and summarize key incidents."*

Within seconds, the AI-generated summary sorted through the noise and highlighted:

- Three login attempts that matched known attack patterns and required immediate action.

- Several false positives, where users were simply logging in from new locations.

- A high-risk phishing attempt targeting the executive team, flagged as a priority threat.

By eliminating unnecessary investigations, Alex's team focused their efforts on real threats, blocking compromised accounts and mitigating a potential breach in minutes.

Reflecting on the experience, Alex realized that Security Copilot wasn't just reducing alert fatigue—it was completely transforming how his security team operated. Instead of chasing endless alerts, they were now working smarter, responding faster, and keeping the company safer with less effort.

Security teams are constantly overwhelmed by alerts, making it difficult to focus on the most pressing threats. AI-powered security tools like Microsoft Security Copilot provide a critical solution, helping organizations:

- Reduce false positives and security alert fatigue.

- Automatically prioritize high-risk threats.

- Generate instant security summaries to streamline investigations.

By leveraging AI-driven threat insights and automated incident response, security teams can operate more efficiently, respond faster, and prevent major security breaches before they happen.

In the next chapter, we'll explore how AI helps predict and mitigate future cyber threats using proactive security intelligence and real-time threat analysis.

# CHAPTER 9: INTEGRATING MICROSOFT SECURITY COPILOT WITH DEFENDER, SENTINEL, AND OTHER SECURITY TOOLS

No single security tool can provide complete protection against the constantly evolving threat landscape. Cyberattacks are becoming more complex, multi-staged, and difficult to detect, often spanning across emails, endpoints, cloud services, and external networks. Organizations need a unified security strategy that consolidates data from multiple security tools, providing real-time threat detection, analysis, and response.

Microsoft Security Copilot serves as a central AI-driven security assistant that integrates with Microsoft's Defender, Sentinel, and Purview security tools, as well as third-party security solutions, to correlate security data, detect sophisticated threats, and automate response actions. By leveraging AI-driven security intelligence, organizations can reduce investigation times, improve threat detection accuracy, and streamline security operations.

In this chapter, we'll explore how Security Copilot enhances Microsoft Defender, Sentinel, and third-party security tools, ensuring a comprehensive and AI-powered defense strategy.

Microsoft Defender is the first line of defense against cyber threats, offering endpoint protection, email security, and cloud security monitoring. However, despite its powerful capabilities, security teams often struggle with:

- Sifting through large volumes of alerts to identify real threats.
- Correlating security signals across multiple devices and users.

- Manually investigating potential breaches to determine the extent of an attack.

Security Copilot enhances Defender's capabilities by using AI-driven insights to improve detection, prioritize threats, and automate response workflows.

For example, when Defender detects suspicious activity on an endpoint, Security Copilot can:

- Analyze the alert in real time and determine whether it's a false positive or an actual attack.

- Correlate the endpoint activity with other security signals, such as phishing emails, cloud access logs, and unusual login attempts.

- Recommend immediate response actions, such as isolating the compromised device, revoking user access, or blocking malicious processes.

By eliminating manual investigation delays, Security Copilot ensures that Defender's security alerts are acted upon instantly, preventing threats from escalating.

While Defender protects individual endpoints and cloud services, Microsoft Sentinel serves as an enterprise-wide security information and event management (SIEM) and security orchestration, automation, and response (SOAR) tool. Sentinel collects security logs from across the organization, providing centralized visibility into security incidents.

Security Copilot takes Sentinel's capabilities further by:

- Correlating security events across multiple systems to identify multi-stage attacks.

- Detecting suspicious patterns that might go unnoticed when reviewing individual alerts separately.

- Automatically generating incident timelines, allowing security analysts to understand the full attack scope within seconds.

For example, if a compromised account is used to access SharePoint, send phishing emails, and execute malicious scripts on an endpoint, Sentinel may detect each event separately. However, Security Copilot can:

1. Correlate these separate events and recognize them as part of a coordinated attack.

2. Identify the attacker's tactics based on historical threat intelligence.

3. Suggest an automated response, such as revoking access, blocking the user, and isolating affected systems.

By integrating Security Copilot with Sentinel, organizations gain a powerful AI-driven security analytics engine that detects sophisticated threats faster and reduces the need for manual investigation.

Many organizations rely on a mix of Microsoft and third-party security tools, such as:

- Firewall solutions (Palo Alto Networks, Cisco, Fortinet) for network security.

- Identity protection tools (Okta, DUO, Ping Identity) for authentication.

- Threat intelligence platforms (Recorded Future, CrowdStrike, FireEye) for external threat detection.

Security Copilot can integrate with these third-party security solutions, ensuring that AI-driven security intelligence is not limited to Microsoft's ecosystem.

For example, by integrating with a third-party firewall, Security Copilot can:

- Analyze traffic patterns and detect signs of malware or data exfiltration.

- Correlate firewall alerts with endpoint activity from Defender and Sentinel.

- Recommend firewall rule changes to automatically block malicious traffic in real time.

This cross-platform security intelligence enables organizations to build a holistic defense strategy that spans across cloud, on-premises, and external security solutions.

One of the most powerful features of Security Copilot is its ability to automate threat correlation across multiple security tools. Instead of security analysts manually piecing together attack patterns, Security Copilot:

- Connects data from Defender, Sentinel, firewalls, identity protection tools, and cloud security platforms.

- Automatically generates attack timelines, showing exactly how an incident unfolded.

- Provides AI-driven recommendations on how to contain the threat and prevent future attacks.

For example, if an employee's device is infected with malware, Security Copilot can:

1. Check if the malware was downloaded through a phishing email detected by Defender for Office 365.

2. Determine if the attacker attempted lateral movement using Sentinel's network logs.

3. Recommend blocking the attacker's IP, isolating the device, and forcing a password reset.

By automating the entire threat investigation process, Security Copilot ensures that security incidents are handled faster, with greater accuracy, and with minimal human intervention.

## Alex's Journey: Creating a Unified AI-Driven Security Strategy for His Company

Alex had spent years working with various security tools, but they always felt disconnected. His SOC team constantly had to switch between Microsoft Defender, Sentinel, firewall logs, and email security platforms, manually correlating data to detect and investigate attacks.

One day, after dealing with a complex security incident involving a phishing attack, an endpoint infection, and a compromised account, Alex realized his team was wasting hours manually connecting security alerts.

Determined to streamline security operations, Alex integrated Security Copilot with his company's entire security stack.

The next time an attack occurred, Security Copilot did the heavy lifting:

- It automatically linked the phishing email to the malware infection, revealing the attack's entry point.

- It detected that the compromised account was being used to access SharePoint, indicating possible data theft.

- It generated a full attack timeline and recommended immediate actions to contain the breach before it escalated.

Instead of manually investigating logs from multiple security tools, Alex's team had a complete attack analysis within seconds.

Security Copilot had transformed their security operations—instead of playing catch-up, they were now proactively preventing attacks and improving their company's overall security posture.

A fragmented security approach makes it difficult to detect, analyze, and respond to sophisticated threats. By integrating Microsoft Security Copilot with Defender, Sentinel, and third-party security tools, organizations can:

- Unify security intelligence across multiple platforms.

- Automate threat correlation, reducing investigation times.

- Improve response accuracy with AI-driven insights.

With AI-powered automation and cross-platform integration, security teams can detect attacks faster, respond more effectively, and proactively strengthen their organization's defenses.

In the next chapter, we'll explore how AI-driven security intelligence is shaping the future of cybersecurity and what organizations can do to stay ahead of evolving threats.

# CHAPTER 10: THE FUTURE OF AI IN CYBERSECURITY – WHAT'S NEXT?

Artificial intelligence has already revolutionized threat detection, security automation, and risk management, but its impact on cybersecurity is just beginning. As cyber threats become more sophisticated, faster, and harder to detect, security teams must stay ahead by leveraging AI-driven security solutions. However, while AI enhances cyber defense strategies, it also brings new challenges, ethical concerns, and the need for human oversight.

AI-driven security solutions like Microsoft Security Copilot are helping organizations automate threat detection, prioritize security incidents, and improve overall security posture. But what does the future hold? How will AI continue to evolve in cybersecurity, and how should security teams prepare for the next wave of AI-powered defense strategies?

This chapter explores the future of AI in cybersecurity, how Generative AI is reshaping security policies, the ethical concerns surrounding AI-driven security, and how organizations can prepare to work alongside AI rather than be replaced by it.

AI is no longer just an add-on to cybersecurity—it is becoming the foundation of modern security strategies. Security teams are moving away from manual, reactive approaches to AI-driven, proactive defense models.

In the near future, AI will play an even greater role in security operations by:

- Predicting cyberattacks before they happen using AI-based threat intelligence.
- Automating nearly all routine security tasks, from alert triage to policy enforcement.

- Detecting zero-day vulnerabilities without needing prior knowledge of attack patterns.

Security Copilot is just one piece of this evolving AI-driven ecosystem, with new capabilities emerging that will allow faster decision-making, more accurate threat detection, and self-healing security environments.

Generative AI, the technology behind large language models (LLMs) like Security Copilot, is reshaping how security teams analyze threats, generate reports, and respond to incidents. Instead of relying on static security playbooks and manual policy updates, AI can:

- Automatically generate security policies based on real-world attack trends.
- Create dynamic security workflows that adapt to new cyber threats in real time.
- Summarize security incidents and create post-attack analysis reports in seconds.

For example, if a new ransomware variant is detected in an organization, Generative AI could:

1. Analyze how the ransomware spreads, identifying weak security controls.
2. Recommend new firewall and endpoint protection rules to contain similar threats.
3. Automatically draft an updated incident response plan, ensuring security teams can react quickly to future attacks.

This shift toward AI-driven security policies and dynamic threat modeling will allow organizations to stay ahead of attackers rather than always reacting to them.

While AI improves security efficiency and response times, it also introduces new challenges and ethical concerns. Security leaders must ask:

- How much decision-making should be automated? AI can detect and respond to threats, but should it have full control over blocking users, isolating devices, or shutting down critical systems?

- How do we prevent AI bias in security decisions? AI models learn from data, but if that data is incomplete or biased, the AI may make flawed security recommendations.

- What are the risks of attackers using AI against organizations? Just as AI can strengthen defenses, cybercriminals are using AI to create more advanced phishing campaigns, deepfake attacks, and AI-powered malware.

Organizations must ensure that AI is used ethically and transparently, keeping humans in the loop for critical security decisions. AI should assist security teams—not replace them.

As AI becomes more embedded in cybersecurity, security teams must adapt their skills and workflows to leverage AI effectively. Instead of fearing that AI will replace human jobs, cybersecurity professionals should focus on mastering AI-driven security tools to enhance their expertise.

Security teams can prepare by:

- Training on AI-driven security platforms like Microsoft Security Copilot, Sentinel, and Defender.

- Shifting from manual alert triage to strategic AI security oversight.

- Developing AI-specific security policies to ensure responsible and effective AI deployment.

Organizations that successfully integrate AI into their security operations will have a significant advantage over those that rely solely on traditional security methods.

## Alex's Journey: Reflecting on How AI Has Transformed His Organization's Security Posture

When Alex first started using Microsoft Security Copilot, he saw it as just another security tool. But over time, he realized that AI was not just assisting his team—it was completely transforming how they operated.

Before Security Copilot, his SOC team was constantly overwhelmed with security alerts, spending hours manually investigating threats, correlating logs, and prioritizing incidents. Now, with AI-driven automation, security response times had dropped from hours to minutes.

Reflecting on his organization's journey with AI-driven security, Alex noticed three key transformations:

1. Incident response was now faster and more accurate – Instead of wasting time on false positives, Security Copilot prioritized real threats and recommended precise response actions.

2. His team was more proactive, not reactive – With AI analyzing trends and predicting threats, his security team had shifted from constantly firefighting to strategic risk prevention.

3. AI-assisted security had freed up time for advanced threat hunting – With Security Copilot handling routine security tasks, Alex's team had time to focus on deeper investigations and security improvements.

As Alex looked ahead, he knew that cybersecurity was evolving rapidly. AI wasn't just a temporary trend—it was the future of security. By embracing AI-driven security solutions, his team had become stronger, smarter, and more efficient—ensuring their organization was better prepared for the cybersecurity challenges of tomorrow.

AI-driven security solutions are shaping the future of cybersecurity, offering faster threat detection, better incident response, and predictive security intelligence. However, organizations must also:

- Address ethical concerns and ensure AI is used responsibly.

- Train security teams to work effectively alongside AI.

- Continuously adapt AI-driven security policies to keep up with evolving cyber threats.

The next decade of cybersecurity will be defined by how well organizations integrate AI into their security operations. Those that successfully adopt AI-driven security strategies will have the upper hand in protecting against modern cyber threats.

With AI as a strategic security ally, organizations can move beyond traditional defense models and create a truly proactive, intelligent cybersecurity strategy.

# BUILDING AN AI-DRIVEN SECURITY STRATEGY FOR THE FUTURE

The rapid evolution of cyber threats demands an equally adaptive and intelligent defense strategy. Organizations can no longer afford to rely on traditional, manual security approaches that struggle to keep up with the speed and complexity of modern cyberattacks. AI-driven security solutions—such as Microsoft Security Copilot—offer a transformational shift in how businesses detect, prevent, and respond to threats.

By integrating AI into security operations, companies gain the ability to detect threats faster, automate repetitive tasks, and make data-driven security decisions. AI is not just a trend in cybersecurity—it is the foundation of the future. However, successful implementation requires a balance between automation and human oversight, ensuring that AI is used responsibly and strategically.

Throughout this book, we explored how AI enhances cybersecurity across multiple areas, from threat detection to compliance, incident response, and insider risk management. Some of the most important lessons include:

- AI-driven threat intelligence allows organizations to detect and respond to attacks faster than traditional security methods.

- Automation reduces security alert fatigue, helping security teams focus on high-risk incidents rather than chasing false positives.

- Integrating Security Copilot with Microsoft Defender, Sentinel, and third-party security tools creates a unified, proactive security strategy.

- AI can assist in meeting compliance requirements by automating security audits, generating reports, and ensuring continuous monitoring.

- Security teams must prepare to work alongside AI rather than fear automation replacing human expertise. AI should complement security analysts, not replace them.

These takeaways reinforce a central theme: Organizations that embrace AI-powered security solutions will have a significant advantage in protecting their data, users, and systems from evolving cyber threats.

While many companies are just beginning to explore AI-powered security, the long-term benefits of integrating AI-driven solutions are clear. Organizations that successfully implement AI-driven security strategies will experience:

1. Faster Threat Detection & Response – AI enables security teams to respond to threats in real-time, significantly reducing the risk of data breaches and operational disruptions.

2. Improved Accuracy & Reduced False Positives – AI analyzes security signals across multiple sources to correlate events and detect real threats, preventing alert fatigue.

3. Automated Compliance & Security Governance – AI helps companies maintain regulatory compliance with automated security monitoring, policy enforcement, and audit reporting.

4. More Efficient Security Teams – Security Copilot and other AI tools reduce manual workloads, allowing teams to focus on proactive threat hunting and strategic security initiatives.

5. Adaptability to Emerging Threats – AI continuously learns from new attack techniques, emerging vulnerabilities, and evolving security trends, ensuring organizations stay ahead of cybercriminals.

While AI is not a silver bullet, it is one of the most powerful tools available to modern security teams. Companies that fail to adopt AI-driven security strategies risk falling behind, facing greater security vulnerabilities, and struggling to defend against increasingly sophisticated attacks.

Adopting AI-driven security is not a one-time event—it requires continuous improvement, adaptation, and strategic planning. Organizations looking to expand their AI-powered security posture should consider the following next steps:

1. Develop an AI Security Roadmap – Assess current security capabilities, identify areas where AI can provide the most value, and establish a long-term implementation strategy.

2. Train Security Teams on AI-Driven Tools – Ensure that SOC teams, IT administrators, and cybersecurity professionals are comfortable using AI-driven security solutions like Security Copilot, Defender, and Sentinel.

3. Refine Security Policies with AI Insights – Use AI-driven analytics to fine-tune DLP rules, insider risk policies, and access controls based on real-world usage patterns.

4. Monitor & Improve AI Effectiveness – Continuously evaluate AI-driven security insights, making adjustments to ensure optimal threat detection and response.

5. Stay Updated on Emerging AI Security Trends – As AI evolves, security teams must stay informed about the latest advancements, threats, and best practices in AI-driven cybersecurity.

AI's role in cybersecurity will continue to grow, and organizations that actively refine and expand their AI-driven security initiatives will remain ahead of the curve.

For Alex, AI was initially just another tool in the ever-expanding security stack. But over time, he realized that Security Copilot and AI-driven security solutions weren't just about automation—they were about transforming how security teams work.

Before implementing AI-driven security strategies, Alex and his team were constantly playing catch-up, manually sifting through alerts, investigating security logs, and responding to incidents reactively. Security felt like an endless battle, with cybercriminals always one step ahead.

However, with Security Copilot and AI-driven security intelligence, things changed.

1. Incident response was faster than ever – Instead of waiting hours to investigate threats, Security Copilot provided instant attack summaries, recommended remediation actions, and automated containment strategies.

2. Threat detection became more proactive – AI-driven insights helped predict and prevent attacks before they happened, shifting the team's focus from reaction to prevention.

3. Security operations became more efficient – AI took over manual security tasks, allowing Alex's team to focus on more complex investigations, strategic planning, and security improvements.

One of the most eye-opening moments for Alex was seeing how AI could detect insider threats before data was exfiltrated. A departing employee attempted to transfer confidential files to a personal cloud storage account. Before Alex's team even noticed, Security Copilot had already blocked the transfer, flagged the user's behavior, and provided a full risk analysis.

Reflecting on his journey, Alex realized that AI wasn't just changing security—it was changing how security professionals work. His team was now smarter, faster, and better equipped to handle cyber threats than ever before.


AI in cybersecurity is no longer optional—it is essential. As cyber threats become more complex, automated, and AI-powered themselves, security teams must embrace AI-driven solutions to stay ahead.

Microsoft Security Copilot represents the next phase of cybersecurity, providing organizations with AI-enhanced threat intelligence, automated security response, and predictive risk analysis.

As we look to the future, AI-driven security strategies will continue to evolve, helping organizations:

- Detect threats faster and with greater accuracy.

- Automate incident response and security operations.

- Strengthen compliance and regulatory readiness.

- Improve overall cybersecurity resilience.

Security professionals and IT leaders who leverage AI-powered security solutions will set their organizations up for success, ensuring stronger defenses, more efficient security teams, and greater protection against emerging cyber threats.

The future of cybersecurity is AI-powered, proactive, and continuously evolving—and those who embrace it will be best prepared for whatever comes next.

www.ingramcontent.com/pod-product-compliance
Lightning Source LLC
LaVergne TN
LVHW052129070326
832902LV00039B/4511